real baby animals
gertie and gus the guinea pigs

by Gisela Buck and Siegfried Buck

For a free color catalog describing Gareth Stevens Publishing's list of high-quality books and multimedia programs, call 1-800-542-2595 (USA) or 1-800-461-9120 (Canada). Gareth Stevens Publishing's Fax: (414) 225-0377. See our catalog, too, on the World Wide Web: http://gsinc.com

Library of Congress Cataloging-in-Publication Data available upon request from publisher. Fax: (414) 225-0377 for the attention of the Publishing Records Department.

ISBN 0-8368-1507-6

First published in North America in 1997 by
Gareth Stevens Publishing
1555 North RiverCenter Drive, Suite 201
Milwaukee, Wisconsin 53212 USA

This edition first published in 1997 by Gareth Stevens, Inc. Original edition © 1993 by Kinderbuchverlag KBV Luzern, Sauerländer AG, Aarau, Switzerland, under the title *Micki und Mucki, zwei kleine Meerschweinchen*. Translated from the German by John E. Hayes. Adapted by Gareth Stevens, Inc. All additional material supplied for this edition © 1997 by Gareth Stevens, Inc.

Photographer: Elvig Hansen
Watercolor artist: Wolfgang Kill
Series editors: Barbara J. Behm and Patricia Lantier-Sampon
Editorial assistants: Diane Laska, Jamie Daniel, and Rita Reitci

Printed in Mexico
1 2 3 4 5 6 7 8 9 01 00 99 98 97

Gareth Stevens Publishing
MILWAUKEE

Guinea pigs come in many different colors and patterns.

This guinea pig will soon give
birth to some babies.

The time has come.

The first baby is born.

Her name is Gertie.

A little later, the second baby
is born. His name is Gus.

Guinea pigs can see, hear, and smell right after they are born.

Gertie and Gus are very hungry.

They nurse, or drink milk from

their mother's body.

When Gertie and Gus finish nursing, they turn over on their backs.

Then their mother licks away their body wastes. In this way, Gertie and Gus stay clean and healthy.

Guinea pigs do not like to be on their own.

When Gertie feels lonely, she squeaks for

her mother.

The mother "mumbles" to let her babies know she is there. The babies answer with a soft "giggle."

Gertie and Gus like to scurry around,
exploring the hay that is their home.

The two little
guinea pigs also
love to play.

Gertie does
a handstand.
Gus does a
somersault.

Gertie and Gus take a daytime nap with their mother, but they are awakened by a noise.

Guinea pigs have very good hearing.

Guinea pigs also sleep during the nighttime hours. Gertie curls up in her little house.

Today, Gertie and her mother snuggle in fresh hay.

Gus also burrows inside the hay.

It feels nice and soft.

Guinea pig teeth are always growing. The teeth wear down when the guinea pigs gnaw on hard objects.

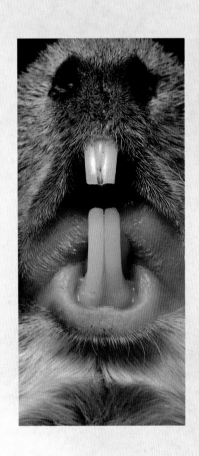

Guinea pigs eat grain, seeds, and bread. And don't forget fresh water!

Gertie and Gus squeak loudly for food when they are hungry. Apples, lettuce, and other vegetables are also part of their varied diet.

Gertie and Gus are two months old now. They are almost fully grown and ready to start families of their own.

Gertie's bright eyes seem to
say that she is ready for new
adventures.

Further Reading and Videos

Babies of the Home. (Grunko Films)

Dazy the Guinea Pig. Jane Burton (Gareth Stevens)

Emily the Traveling Guinea Pig. Smith (Astor-Honor)

The Guinea Pig. (Encyclopædia Britannica Educational Corporation)

Guinea Pigs. Barrett (Franklin Watts)

Guinea Pigs. Evans (Dorling Kindersley)

Guinea Pigs Far and Near. Duke (Dutton)

Hazel the Guinea Pig. Wilson (Candlewick Press)

See How They Grow. (Children's Television International)

Taking Care of Your Guinea Pig. Pope (Franklin Watts)

Tell Me Why: Mammals. (Prism Video)

Your First Guinea Pig. Steinkamp (TFH Publications)

Fun Facts about Guinea Pigs

Did you know . . .

— guinea pigs are rodents, and aren't related to pigs at all?

— guinea pigs live in the wild in South America?

— guinea pigs are very clean and tidy pets?

— guinea pigs make a loud, whistling sound when they are frightened?

— guinea pigs have no tails?

— guinea pigs live an average of eight years?

— wild guinea pigs live in tunnels they dig in the ground?

Glossary-Index

body wastes — the urine and excrement produced by animals as the end result of the digestive processes (p. 9).

burrow (v) — to hide or conceal oneself; to snuggle (p. 17).

explore — to look around or investigate in order to discover what is there (p. 12).

gnaw — to chew on something that is very hard without intending to eat it. Rodents must gnaw often because their front teeth never stop growing. The gnawing keeps their teeth trimmed down to a useful size (p. 18).

handstand — the act of standing with the hands or paws on the ground and the body and legs up in the air (p. 13).

hay — cut and sometimes dried grass, clover, and other plants. It is used for food and bedding for various animals (pp. 12, 16, 17).

nap (n) — a short sleep, usually during the day (p. 14).

nurse — to drink the milk produced by a female mammal's body (pp. 8, 9).

pattern — a design (p. 2).

scurry — to run very quickly in various directions (p. 12).

snuggle — to curl up cozily or comfortably (p. 16).

somersault — a roll on the ground, turning in a complete circle from head to feet (p. 13).

squeak — to make a short, shrill cry or noise (p. 10).